a-"Word"

a-"Word"

Sol Goldberg, M.D.

VANTAGE PRESS
New York

It is hoped by the author that after reading this book, people who have had problems with a loss of a similar nature (and there has to be an enormous number of them) will realize their response to tragedy is normal and shared with others and, as such, will benefit accordingly.

FIRST EDITION

Published by Vantage Press, Inc.
516 West 34th Street, New York, New York 10001

Manufactured in the United States of America
ISBN: 0-533-11905-7

Library of Congress Catalog Card No.: 96-90137

0 9 8 7 6 5 4 3 2 1

Dedication

This book is dedicated to Ruth, my beloved wife of sixty-one years, until "God" took her from me. We often dressed alike at affairs to give the guests a laugh and were known as "the twins."

We took thirty-one cruises and we won thirty-one costume prizes due to her talents. She was a wonderful asset to me and everyone she touched benefitted from her. Nothing was too hard to do nor too much. Impossible meant to try a bit harder. The first time we went to Hawaii she was shown the hula and from that time on she became enamored with the culture and became an excellent Hawaiian dancer and entertained in numerous shows with her cohorts.

She never considered herself to be an artist, yet her work was outstanding with many original ideas. She won prizes in six different categories in art and as such has one at the present time upon the wall of the Cedars Sinai Hospital in Los Angeles, California.

She went to only one writing class and was voted the best in the class. Her teacher called me recently to ask if she could present her writing as the best she had ever had. Everything she did was the best!

We were fortunate to have three wonderful sons:

Sanford, an outstanding attorney in Beverly Hills, California; Dennis, an outstanding medical physician in Coeur d'Alene, Idaho; and Terry, a prominent lawyer in Encino, California. All three are delightful and full of fun. Their offspring rendered no less than two excellent attorneys, one fine teacher, and one professor-physician. The rest of the herd are young and on their way to prominence because nothing is too hard, nor too tough to do. With effort, everything can be accomplished.

Dedication to the younger generation includes: grandchildren: Bradley, Brian, and twins Lauren and Linda, Allison, Todd and Jessica.

Last but not least, to my six great-grandchildren:
Sarah and Benjamin,
Joshua and Danielle,
Lily and Joy Rachel.

All are a delight and ones to love, hold, and depend upon.

Also a thanks to a longtime friend, Helen Harris, and a special thanks to Ellen Leonard, M.P.A. for her critique and review of my text.

Contents

Foreword

The pages in this small book were never intended to become a book; I wrote them in a release of tension on my computer at the death of my dear wife, Ruth. They described my inner feelings with my great loss.

Some documents were strewn around my desk and an occasional friend or relative would read them and remark how true my response to loss was. They felt these should be published so others would realize that they are not unique in their response to grief.

At first I declined to submit them to a publisher. My feelings were personal and so profound. Basically, I am an "up-person" and didn't want to share my grief with others. With much persuasion, I allowed forty words to be submitted to a publisher and I was still not desirous of having my feelings in print for others to read. To my surprise the editor felt that this book should be available for others, which should console some to realize their feelings are shared in a loss.

My training in medicine in the Los Angeles County Hospital during the thirties, the Depression Period, with wards of fifty patients or more, allowed me to see the lonely, the morose, the impoverished and the dying. Some were crying, smoking, masturbating, singing, hallucinating, and others screaming and tied down. I, as a young physician, was sure that I would find all the answers to disease and cure everyone.

I watched, helped or occasionally delivered babies with the resident physician standing by in the Bunker Hill area in Los Angeles, California. Newspapers and rags on crate boxes substituted for a delivery table or bed. When I came back the next day to examine the new mother and baby she was out hanging the wash and said, "Go away, man. I have no time to talk to you." And she meant it. I had to repeat similar reports with negative examination. Statistics were incomplete.

My early private practice as a general practitioner was a one-man clinic with a charge of one dollar "on the books" for examination and treatment. I was open until late at night hoping a drop-in patient would pay a dollar for care. My wife acted as my nurse.

One night a patient paid up his bill of eight dollars for eight prior treatments. That was my biggest fee to date. I was elated. My wife and I took a patient and her husband out for ice cream sundaes to celebrate—cost fifteen cents each—I left a twenty-five-cent tip for all to see in the center of the table. I was a sport. I never felt I was poor—I just didn't have any money.

My change from a general practitioner to a plastic surgeon was the responsibility of an alcoholic patient, M.B. Almost every weekend she became intoxicated and came in bleeding with injuries from a fall. I sewed her up and she was a fine healer with practically no scar results. One day she came into the office and said that I was going to do a face-lift on her. I asked, "What is a face-lift?" That's how little was known about plastic surgery at the time. She had a previous face-lift in Chicago and showed me the minimal scars she had in her hair. I said, "I will not."

She said to me, "You have the hands and the skills to become a plastic surgeon."

I said, "No way."

She next said, "I will give you a lot in Hemet for the procedure."

I said, "I will do it." I would now be a property owner. I did not know where Hemet was at the time.

She described the procedure to me. I then read every article there was at the time to learn the technique. Arrangements were made and she drew the locations of the incisions on her scalp at the elected time for the surgery.

I, in my meager quarters and limited instruments, with my wife as an acting nurse, proceeded to perform the first face-lift I witnessed.

An excellent result was obtained and I then proceeded to obtain training with a noted plastic surgeon, Dr. T. Floyd Brown. That was the beginning of my specialty. Additional training followed until I became board certified in plastic surgery.

This is a brief background of my past writings or accolades:

1. Listed in the book *Marquis Who's Who in the West*, eighth edition, Library of Congress Catalog Card Number 49-48186, page 266.

2. "Diminishing Facial Wrinkles by Linear Eversion," *Archives of Otolaryngology* 90 November 1969, copyright American Medical Association.

3. "The Subtleties of Facial Injuries in P.I. Cases," *Advocate,* June 1978.

4. "Undetected Nasal Fractures in Personal Injury Cases," *California Trial Lawyers Association Forum,* October 1979.

5. "The Cicatrix [Scar] due to Trauma," *Advocate,* January 1980.

6. "Rhytidectomy Made Simple," *Advocate,* September 1980.

7. "Latent Nasal Deformities Resulting from Trauma," *Advocate,* December 1980.

8. Participated in the educational program cosponsored by the American Board of Cosmetic Plastic Surgery. I described various techniques of suturing wounds—1982.

9. American Medical Association Physicians Recognition Award, 1982.

10. Certification in continuing medical education—California Medical Association, 1983.

11. "The Use of Hypothermia in Surgery," *Medical Journal,* 1982.

12. "The Simple Approach to the Nasal Tip," *Medical Journal,* 1983.

13. "The Double 'V' for the Double Chin," *Medical Journal,* 1983.

14. Voted physician emeritus, Hollywood Community Hospital, 1984.

15. Certificate of Approval to Supervise Plastic Surgeons for Approval, Hollywood Community Hospital, Hollywood, California.
16. American Medical Association Physicians Recognition Award, 1985.
17. "Plastic Surgery for Traumatic Injuries," *Advocate*, March 1987.
18. "The Psychological and Physiological Aspects of Facial Scars," *Advocate*, 1989.
19. American Medical Association Physician's Recognition Award, September 1, 1993.
20. Los Angeles County Medical Association Membership, 1996.
21. Medical Board of California License, 1996—number AFE 26979.
22. Member of American Medical Association.
23. Member of California Board of Certification in Plastic Surgery since October 29, 1962—number 154.
24. Member of Association for Medical Specialty in Plastic Surgery since August 13, 1969—number 85.

Graduate, University of California, Irvine—M.D. degree, 1933, license no. AFE 26975.

Memberships:

Stephen S. Wise Temple
Los Angeles Museum of Art
Ionic Masonic Lodge #520 F. and A.M.

Ionic Golf Club
Westchester Masonic Lodge #572 F. and M.
San Bernardino Scottish Rite Temple
Westwood Shriners, Los Angeles, California
Licensed Real Estate Broker, State of California

Background

I was one of seven children, with five sisters and one brother.

I was third from the eldest. My father was rarely home and it behooved me to be the man of the house. What that meant I did not really know. When I was a youngster we moved so many times I never had any friends. I went from one school to another once for only one week.

I remember working at the Los Angeles Coliseum at the age of thirteen selling Eskimo Pies (ice-cream bars covered with chocolate). I walked up and down so many stairs I felt I could reach Mount Everest. On a good day, I earned about two dollars!!!

I worked there during the 1932 Olympics and was thus able to see the great Wykoff run the hundred-meter race to victory.

I worked my way through school as a truck driver for a paper company. I had to load, then deliver merchandise and return the truck for two dollars a day after school. It included wrapping paper and cases of toilet paper. I guess it made me strong.

I used to read the dictionary when I was alone and

occasionally write a story. I wish I knew what they were at that time.

I met my loving wife, Ruth, in 1931. We were together for the rest of her life.

We formed a "Big Doers" club of boys and girls and had much fun with a number of friends. There were several piano players, singers and dancers, and just funsters. I was made the first president of the group at the age of eighteen. We all had a lot of fun going to the beach or someone's house and just singing or talking or dancing.

I went to Los Angeles High School and lettered in the Class C Basketball Group (small ones of up to 110 pounds). I was the handball champion in college.

As a bowler, I won many nonprofessional championships. I entered the Examiner Tournament with a throng of 25,000 and came in second. I beat Ned Day, the current champion at the time, and the Pico Palace offered me a professional rating to represent them in the major tournaments. This I refused as I was actively engaged in the practice of medicine.

I used to ride a horse at Griffith Park each Sunday for five years. It was fun getting there and hearing Kataba neighing as I approached.

I was encouraged to try my luck and skill at golf. I was very successful and won the championship at the Masonic Lodge a number of times, also low gross in the Stuntman's Outing. I entered a professional golf tournament, The Montebello Open, and qualified with a 74. I did not believe I could do that well against the pros, so I had an officeful of patients the next day and could not continue to play. I was lucky to have had two holes in one. The last one was at Rancho Park, the twelfth hole, in 1993.

I am only telling this as Vantage Press asked me to tell you a bit of my background. This is not to brag, as everything took a lot of effort. I am lucky, as pressure is part of my life, which is an aid in sports.

My wife and I attended most of the Westwood Shrine affairs and many members would wait to see what my wife and I wore. We were known as "the Twins," as we dressed alike for the occasions. We danced at all the affairs and were the last ones to leave. People that were unable to dance often told us that we were the Ginger Rogers and Fred Astaire couple of the Shriners.

At anyone's birthday my wife would call up and ask for the birthdayite and say, "Western Union is calling." When they answered I would play "Happy Birthday" on the harmonica, often followed by "Jingle Bells." They always appreciated it. We all had fun.

Approximately two years ago our life suddenly changed. We were coming home from the Friars Club one evening in Beverly Hills, California when I opened the door to our house. We were pushed in from behind, not permitted to turn around, with a gun pressed against my head by the masked and capped holdup man. He said in a quiet voice, "Give me all your jewels and money." We quickly responded with the removal of jewelry which we had worn for the lavish occasion. Then he said, "Take me back to your safe," which we did not have, but we went to the back of the house and

I opened boxes with no jewels and suddenly he disappeared. He must have rushed for a driver to pick him up. The fear that was present never ceased and we had protection from the Bel Air patrol every time we came into the house.

Two weeks later on a sunny Sunday afternoon with neighbors washing cars and trimming plants, the doorbell rang. I opened the door and screamed as another huge hood stood there with a gun at my face. I screamed so loudly he was scared off, and my wife heard my scream. She almost passed out. Fears mounted and shortly thereafter she became acutely ill, with nurses around-the-clock, and finally succumbed.

Shortly thereafter I was stricken and emergency bypass surgery was performed. Prior to these horrible tragedies I would play golf, walk, carry my clubs, and have energy left to wash both our automobiles. Sometimes I would even work in the yard at night and trim a tree or two.

Now it is all changed. I moved to a condominium alone. Energy has waned and with great effort I am trying to do things and play golf again, this time with a cart, as I cannot walk and play as before.

Society has had an effect on my life. I am still going to continue as best I can. I am strong-willed. The impossible is more difficult but hopefully attainable.

Grief

Grief can be defined as "deep mental suffering." When one experiences a great loss, as the loss of a long-standing, wonderful, talented, beautiful, helping mate, grief becomes a constant, undesirable pal.

This pal is tenacious and won't let go.

Try as you might, this pal won't disappear.

There are days when this pal is in hiding, but sooner or later this pal appears, often times with increased intensity. All "hell" breaks loose with "giant" tears and "sobbing" that tends to wrench all your guts out. You cry shamelessly. Your eyes feel as though they are going to burst and pop out of your head. Your vision is impaired, you feel helpless, and any voluntary motion seems so difficult. Eating is only because of habit and necessity. Your weight drops. Your head seems so full and painful. Even your ears are clogged and hearing reduced. The anguish is enormous.

This feeling is so strong that you feel as though you are going to die and often wish you would. It may last for many hours or even days. You cannot avoid it. Here comes your unwanted "pal." You want to scream and often do. You feel so helpless.

You are smart enough to know that no one lasts

forever and the end finally takes us all. But for the living and remaining spouse, the pal won't go away.

Speaking with other unfortunate ones that have also lost a desirable mate, they say this pal does not come that often or stay as long and often visits with less intensity, but never leaves permanently. Wish we could choose only the "pals" we want.

Vision

Vision can refer to many things, including the ability to see, an image created by the mind, exceptional discernment, and a lovely sight.

What a great word.

You can apply this to: Einstein, a German-born American physicist who had great knowledge of electricity as a start, leading up to the atomic bomb and beyond with the theory of relativity, the earliest flying machine as a single-seater, being pulled by hand or propelled by feet as a start of our everyday airplanes; Henry Ford with the early automobile, cranking it as a way to start it on its merry way.

These are but a few thoughts relating to this word "vision." Young boys or young girls as they mature may think of the types of persons they would like to be. The field of endeavor as a life's work; whom they would like to meet and marry some day. They follow this with thoughts of a family with their future children to enhance their home life. They may think of doing sports with the children or studying with them so they will all be huge successes. The type of car they would like, or fancy clothes they would enjoy were all part of their vision. They may see themselves as the most prominent person in the world, a president, a doctor or a lawyer. They dream they may change the world to become an ideal place for all mankind with plenty for all without fraud and pollution. What a great dream to have and it is essential for progress.

All this is a fine approach to life. However is there one thought that any interruption of the dream could be terminated due to illness or death? One must in one's quest for success realize illness or death comes to us all in due time.

This should not deter one from achieving success and accomplishing one's dream. It makes it worth one's while for one's existence.

Lonely

Lonely: bereft, lacking companionship, sad from being alone.

This is only a beginning explanation as to how one feels at the loss of a treasured lifetime mate.

The walls tremble often with eerie sounds. And other times the quiet becomes deafening as one imagines and tries to hear the absent spouse.

You hear voices, which reverberate, but only in one's mind. Shadows fall and vibrate with every breath of the remaining individual, imagining the lost one is trying to tell you something. You respond with talking out loud to yourself. You are shameless as the desire to communicate with the deceased is overwhelming. Sensations of an eerie nature overcome you.

Frightening sounds or motions about you are often either felt or really heard.

You sometimes believe that you are seeing or feeling the lost individual and find yourself talking out loud. You almost feel foolish and yet you try to believe contact has been made. How difficult now is.

Being alone with only walls to talk to gives you a weird sensation of communication with the dead or the notion that your mind is actually telling you tales that are hard to believe.

It's wonderful and frightening at the same time.

I sometimes think that I am losing my mind.

I try to think of all the lonely people in the world and feel so sorry for them. It is tragic to be alone unless that is your normal preference. But, for the remaining mate of a long happy marriage, the desolation hurts so deeply that you often cannot speak as the pressure in your throat and chest overwhelms you to such a point that you feel that you can barely breathe. You hate, hate, hate, your new life of being alone. In time you will have some relief and move forward as is the usual custom.

Pick yourself up, seek new activities.

With effort you can succeed and the effort will be worthwhile with newfound friends.

Feelings

We think of feelings as sensory experiences, including emotional ones, passions, affections.

After the loss of someone so very dear for many years these words hardly touch or accentuate these symptoms.

A void is created with the depth of feeling so great as to be devastating. You feel alone with friends and relatives all around lending support. Two hundred cards of condolence have some but minimal meaning as the void is so traumatic.

No one can imagine how another feels in the loss of a loved one. The tender care and love that has prevailed and even increased with time is now gone.

A touch, a word, a feeling of being someone and being with someone, is now only a dream.

You now live only with walls about you, almost a feeling of being in jail, even though you are now free as a bird to go and come as you please.

You do not wish to go and come as you please. You can only cry for your loved one, whom you can no longer touch or feel. How sad. "God" did not design life in a proper manner. He should have had consultation.

Time

Time has many definitions. These are but a few: duration, epoch, period.

Why waste it? It can never be retrieved.

One must utilize it to the best of one's ability as it cannot be replaced.

It is one of the most valuable assets given to us. Some are limited in it, while others are more fortunate to live long. The richest person cannot buy it or extend it.

How we utilize it to get the most benefit from it is up to us. With our given time, we are able to waste it, which is a shame, or use it to our advantage and grow.

The saying "time marches on" is very real.

Most successful people have found that they do not have enough time to accomplish all their goals. This is unfortunate as society might benefit from their activities.

Many research doctors can only add to the present knowledge without ever attaining their goal. Jonas Salk, who discovered the "polio" vaccine, is working feverishly on a potential vaccine to prevent malignancies. His time is running out. Hope he succeeds again.

I am limited in time at the moment, so I say to all,

"Utilize your time to the best of your ability so when your time is up you will have accomplished as much as you were able."

Hobby

A hobby can be a toy, a relaxing activity, or an interest. It could be a wooden horse on a merry-go-round. To some people their work is their hobby.

Some people never have a hobby.

Many countries abhor playing and only know work as a lifestyle. They are controlled by their customs and any form of a hobby is taboo.

A hobby can mean many things to different people. Some only have a hobby as a lifestyle. I believe their lives are unfulfilled.

It seems to me that people should have hobbies as it gives them a release from their routine lifestyle. Even though they may enjoy their work as a complete way of living, they could be more interesting people for at least having tried one.

As we all know, there are many types of hobbies; however, fishing and golf seem to attract the majority.

One must, however, never become so engrossed in a hobby that one neglects one's work, family, and friends. That is one of the evils of a hobby. When it overwhelms the individual, he or she may lose contact with the real world.

Hobbies are wonderful. I have tried many with a

certain amount of success. One feels a sense of accomplishment just to try a new hobby. It is healthy for the mind as well as the body and gives one a sense of satisfaction.

It is the learning process that can be very rewarding and tends to counterbalance the trials of living in a competitive world. One may find that in some cases the almighty dollar is not the most important goal in one's life.

Enough, another time I will expound further.

Keen

Keen: pungent, intensely sharp, quick-witted, eager, responsive, a lament.

Certainly a word of multiple choices.

A better thought is to determine how it might apply to you. Stating "that is keen" could mean so many things. It could indicate that it is sharp, great, fun, exciting, desirable, etc. A keen mind is one that is exploring, knowledgeable, investigating new products and studious, often trying to keep up or get ahead of the new trends.

Someone might say, "Isn't she or he keen?" meaning smart, very nice, lovable, attractive, and desirable.

A keen mind is never satisfied and is hungry for improvement, one that is always exploring or trying to get ahead of progress. The problem with such a person is that one is often limited in social activities because one cannot tolerate the lesser or slower-responding mind in another.

Usually this individual goes on to higher education and now may be confronted with other, keener-minded individuals. The desire for knowledge is often so great at the expense of one's health. "Watch it."

Sometimes because of greater competition with

added stress, this person may tend to fall back and not do his/her best in school or other activities. This then becomes a trauma, which is not easily tolerated. One may drift from the mainstream of things and become unhappy without the determination to further develop oneself. It takes a strong individual to be second fiddle to a smarter keener mind. If you have good friends, keep them for their other good qualities, which you enjoy.

It is up to you if the reverse is your situation. Do the best you can.

You also have to be tolerant of the lesser-minded ones and help them. Their friendship will be your reward.

Lease

A lease is a legal document conveying property for a specific time—an opportunity for continuance of such rights—a new lease on life.

This suggests to me that you may lease some thing or object, as a car, for a period of time. At the end of the period of the lease, you return the object. It may be an automobile, a computer, or even a life. It must be returned.

In one instance you have the option to renew the lease under certain conditions or even purchase the object. In the case of a life, it must be returned to "God" without any stipulation on your part.

One has to consider that a life is only on a lease basis. In time we must all give up our lease on life.

This should make us decide at a very early age what we should do with the time allotted to us. Let us be good and kind, as most individuals need help.

It often seems futile to advance one's efforts to the extreme in order to get the most out of life.

To develop oneself to the utmost, realizing every day your lease is running out, seems futile.

The irony is that the ones who have the most to

contribute to this world have so little time and are never able to give their all.

By the time one has really developed one's talents, the lease starts to run out.

A mate of long standing who is taken away when the lease expires leaves a terrible void in the remaining spouse. The depth of this loss is one of the greatest pains a normal person can feel. Sobbing only partly alleviates the feeling, crying does not help much, but cannot be avoided. Maybe time will diminish the torture of loss when the lease runs out.

Philosophy

Philosophy can be defined as "an organized body of thought; a way of viewing the world; an exploration of knowledge by speculative means."

Life is a very interesting experience.

A child is conceived.

How do I react to this world of ours?

I was in an enclosed area, unable to see, but I think I could feel, as I was pushed around from time to time. I felt like I was in an ocean with a storm in progress and became dizzy at times. I vomited on occasion, I think, and bounced around a lot.

At first I had no ears, eyes, bones and other materials or organs that later developed. I didn't even have a brain. I resented a lot of things and at first could not complain too much, but as time went on and I grew a little, I started to move a lot and then I even kicked.

On several occasions when I was entombed, I could feel a ray of electricity or other beam to form my sex organs and I tried to see if they were on straight. What are sex organs? Do you play it or does it make music and squeal like a mouse, which I never saw?

Can you imagine my chagrin when so many things happen to me and I have nothing to say? Even though

I can't talk, I still have feelings, I think. I think I can think. I could go on and on, but to where? Where did I come from? Can you imagine that I'm so tiny, alone, in a riverbed of sperms that are darting about trying to jump me when I was just looking for a place to rest my body, which I did not have. I looked and looked and finally found a place to set my weary bones, which I also did not have. A sperm finally struck me and forced me up against a wall, which stuck to me till I was born. Could you think that an unknown of my size could unite with something? A sperm to which I was never properly introduced. Maybe I was introduced, but had nothing to say. Is that fair?

My whole life is a mystery to me and I wonder what I was before?

Faith

The dictionary says: it is a constant belief, trust, belief in "God," religious conviction; loyalty, and allegiance.

How about faith in oneself?

How important for one to say, "I can do it."

One must believe in oneself. How important it is to say, "I did it myself."

To have a belief in "God" is a wonderful thing. It gives one something to believe in, to console one, and yes, someone to talk to. But you are the one I am talking to in this message.

To talk or think about something you want to do or be and do nothing about it because of fear that you may not succeed is certainly not the way to live.

You must try to do the things you believe in and make every effort to succeed in your endeavors. Make the most of yourself. Develop your talents and continue to seek new goals. Your faith in yourself will grow continuously.

Failure is not failure unless you never try to do the things you should do to make them work.

The failure is in not trying.

You must have faith in yourself that you can do it to succeed in life.

Only from thoughts do great things originate and by persistence, development follows.

Well, enough lecture. Get out and try for whatever goal you wish and good things will happen. Have faith in yourself that you will succeed and that is success in itself.

Goal

A goal is a purpose, a conclusion, a means of scoring in certain sports, an aim, etc.

This is a message for all to read.

To be happy in this world of ours, one must accomplish one's own goals.

For a youngster growing up and pondering what route to follow, it is always a problem as to what is the field for one. It is essential that one look around and see what avenue might suit one's attributes. Remember I am writing to a youth who has not decided on any direction as yet.

Life is not all fun and games and work is a part of the process. If school is the direction for you, then you must find the field that you think you might be happy in. Try different subjects to get an idea to see if the field of study excites you. If so, that study will be a welcome challenge and fun. Always think that you are the one who might find the answer to the unknown question in our universe. Whatever field you like, there is an unknown quantity to be discovered.

If things are given to you on a silver platter, that is fine; but personal accomplishment is the final challenge.

I would like to say if you realize your goal, you are a rare individual. To succeed one must now find another goal and so forth to keep the brain and body in harmony.

Always look ahead for further development and you will never be bored. Take life as a game, win only the honorable way, and you will be happy. Possessions are nice but never in themselves bring happiness. Your own accomplishment should be your goal for the zest of life. Be tolerant of others of lesser talents, the aged and infirmed, and you will have an emotionally happy life.

Talent

Talent has been defined as "a special skill; a flair; a type of ancient currency."

What a waste if one does not use or develop one's given talent. One with lesser ability can often excel over the one with talent who does not develop it.

A talent can be noticed in the way a mother cares for a child, to bring out the best in the infant so that he/she can find one's place in society.

An artist without desire can only apply paint to a canvas. One with less ability who strives for betterment can often excel over the talented one.

An athlete with talent and desire becomes a saint to the underlings and just to touch him, or get an autograph, is a great delight to many.

One with lesser athletic prowess can still enjoy and bring out one's best potential. This should give one a sense of accomplishment. The talented musician at a very early age can be recognized throughout the world, but, without the desire to maintain his/her finest ability one soon fades. As a talented musician has said, "If I don't practice for one day, I notice it; if I don't practice for two days, the public notices it."

It shows that talent without the desire to excel

could be a waste without the effort it takes to develop it and stay on top. One with a lesser talent can still perform a similar type of art and enjoy it with the feeling of a job well done.

So, if you're talented in a certain field and enjoy it, develop it to the fullest for all to enjoy.

If you are less or not talented and enjoy a certain activity, do the best you can and be thankful for the opportunity to try. That is worth a lot.

Fall

The dictionary says that fall has numerous meanings. A few are now given: to descend; to die in warfare; to err or sin; to assume a place; to hang loosely; to occur by chance.

Some of these meanings may apply to everyone.

Imagine one falling in or out of love. You can fall out of line. A fall into line might apply to those who have deviated from the straight and narrow path.

Lifestyles usually change with a fall in income. One must be able to adjust to maintain a satisfactory response.

Niagara Falls is a phenomenon of nature beautiful to behold.

One can fall down but must pick oneself up.

A fall in temperature can give you a chill.

In fall the trees lose their leaves, but in spring they return with new vigor and blossoms. Some come with fruit for your liking.

A number of these thoughts may apply to you and only you can lift yourself up from a fall. You can start with a fresh beginning just as the deciduous trees do each spring.

So—if you have fallen—only you can spring back. It takes self-discipline and effort.

So—good luck.

If you have not fallen, helping someone who has may be very rewarding for you.

Looking forward to spring and the beautiful change in temperature and colors gives me pep to refresh myself and to start anew.

New vistas will be mentioned in another one of my philosophies.

Proofread

Proofread means to read and correct and/or improve. Just imagine if we could proofread our own actions before we do them. We are placed upon this earth without any previous knowledge, yet we have to make decisions as we go along. Many times we have to make monumental decisions without any previous experience or knowledge. How is it possible to be correct each and every time?

As children growing up, we are taught by parents or elders right from wrong. Sometimes they are not sure themselves. They often tend to direct our future in work or marriage, not knowing our capacity to accept that lifestyle.

We have to make lifetime goal decisions as youngsters, not knowing what the future will bring. Imagine a child saying, "I want to be a doctor or lawyer when I grow up," with no knowledge of what it really means.

We cannot proofread our futures.

Should we marry? A question we all ask ourselves as youngsters and only being part of a family allows us to make the decisions. No two families are alike. We cannot proofread the future. Life is full of anxieties and dilemmas as we try to find our rightful spot in society.

We must continually make decisions without adequate knowledge. The Peter Principle exists for all of us, but where is the limit of development?

If we could proofread all our activities in life and act accordingly, we might live an entirely different life than we have and be much happier with the change.

Too bad we cannot proofread our lifestyle before it happens so that we could avoid the errors that we make. This would allow us to come up to our greatest potential, be happier, and contribute our finest efforts toward mankind.

Mischievous

This means playful in a destructive or annoying way.

To begin with, it is a difficult word to spell. It is easier to spell it wrong than right.

Some people feel that they are cute when they are mischievous. They could be clever to a fault, trying to play a trick on someone who they know cannot take a joke.

In reality it is not funny to make a goat out of anyone.

It is only enjoyable to the culprit trying to be funny and could actually create harm.

Do not interpret a cute joke as being mischievous unless it is harmful.

I am trying to be funny at this time with the computer, but it only responds to my input without feelings. I cannot take credit for any funny or mischievous act an inanimate object does, as it does not respond emotionally.

There is some type of thrill in a mischievous act and if no harm is done, it can be cute and enjoyable to all concerned.

So go ahead and connive a clever innocuous trick and enjoy the exciting result. If you are good at it, you might become a comedian for all to enjoy.

Power

Power indicates strength, control, political influence, or a source or degree of energy.

Power often goes to one's head.

A citizen of a country may become the president. This sudden power could tend to destroy his or her judgment. They often forget the little man or woman.

The new president now has the "power" to control lives. This office allows one to almost become a dictator. It is true they have some control in Congress and the Senate in our country.

The office allows one to bring us to the brink or actually be involved in war, often against the thinking of the average citizen. Hostages are released or kept according to relations with foreign enemies. The president is actually involved.

Our own president now is trying to control women's rights for abortion without regard to the factors involved. He is not a physician nor psychiatrist. It is not his business to interfere with lives. A physician is better qualified.

Power gives one an ego beyond one's imagination.

Control of a vehicle gives one power, which is exhibited in the way they drive. "Me first always" is the way some people drive. Raising one's voice is a way to gain power. An example would be Adolf Hitler, a terrible tyrant.

A great actor or actress can hold an audience in his or her power with but a twinkle of the eye, a raising of an eyebrow or a slight gesture.

Money has a great effect on some with wealth. They want you to feel inferior, as it gives them power.

Well, I could go on but I am going to lunch. With my power to end this jargon, I am closing.

Enough

To put it simply, enough means "sufficient" or "adequate."

What is enough?

When you are hungry, only food is your want. When you are thirsty, water is your only desire. For an athlete, winning and a new record is the goal.

If you are short, you want to be tall.

If you are very tall, you want to be shorter.

One is never satisfied with one's body. If one is pretty or handsome, one wants to be prettier or more handsome, or if self-conscious, then one does not want to be good looking.

If one has dimples, one usually does not want them and those without may envy those who have.

The structure of bodies varies and envy of another is almost always present.

If a child has a toy and sees other children with toys, the first child wants the other children's toys and vice versa.

The wealthy want to be wealthier and even the wealthiest wants to have more.

The dictionary states that "enough" means as much as satisfies. That is the question. "What is enough?"

Want

Want is defined as "To desire; wish for. To need or require, also quality lacking."

When you are young, you want your mother's breast. You are hungry or need security.

Growing up you need parents', friends' or teachers' help. As a teenager you begin to need the association of the opposite sex. Your life's goal is next. Some now want only luxuries.

Nothing is quite good enough. Whatever others have, you want, or even better, to outdo them. Luxuries are the theme of the times. Buy and replace, as the desires are now in command.

Change of clothes, cars, yes, and even homes are the present desire. Whatever someone else has or does must be outdone. This becomes a problem as the real life's needs are completely forgotten.

The desire for wealth increases. The strain mounts in the home as the individuals are often pressed beyond capabilities to keep up with the "Joneses." Families suffer. I do not blame people for wanting nice things and improvements, but too often at a great price.

It is healthy to want to improve one's station and position in life. But when is enough, enough?

Enough criticism. Without dreams and desires to excel, progress would be at a standstill. We would not have the luxuries in a home, automobile or office. We take for granted the radio, the television, the fax machine, automation, etc. The original computer made by IBM took up an entire room with very limited capacity compared to even the laptop computer today. When is the last time a "Yippie" saw the sun, the moon, the stars and smelled a rose? Try it sometimes. It might be a revelation.

As one gets older, the want takes on a new meaning. To be without pain, able to do one's own chores, maintain one's faculties, being able to get out on one's own is a great triumph. In many cases with extreme effort. A "plaque" should be given to the aged for their efforts to "want" to survive and be independent.

Destruction

What is it really?

We could say it is utter ruin—for living things, death.

An earthquake with a power of 7.2 can and does destroy anything in its path.

A tidal wave can come ashore and envelop anything on its course. A tornado produces great havoc in its pathway.

One must realize that the previous statements are true facts. Now comes another side of the term "destruction."

This is the one you and I can do something about.

A drunken individual behind the wheel of an automobile can cause serious injury and even death.

Yelling at a spouse or child in one's home is a serious matter. When things do not go right, discussing the problem at hand might be a better way to solve a situation. The excitement of a loud voice can be emotionally destructive, which could have a lasting effect. A child growing up in this atmosphere could be devastated. Even a look askance can be harmful to the recipient of this act, which can be traumatic.

Any loud noise, such as blowing the horn of an automobile can be harmful.

Overindulgence is destructive, as one is never satisfied. Thus we can see, there are different types of destruction, those that nature provides and those that man delivers. We cannot avoid nature's wrath, only man's.

Soul

We know the soul as the intangible essence of an individual.

It is the moving spirit of the person.

It is the seat of emotion, of sentiment.

The center of mortal powers.

We can be endowed with either a gilded soul or tainted soul. The person with the gilded soul has an aura around him or her that is lustrous and subtly evident to most whom he/she encounters. Such individuals exude a gleaming atmosphere and a loving expression. They give off a beautiful light so that even the hostile individual they might meet is often inspired with awe.

The person with the tainted soul is one who is impregnated with a poisonous attitude.

Such persons seem to be infected with incipient putrefaction. To change their plight or predicament would benefit them and make life more pleasant.

We cannot all have gilded souls, but to strive toward that goal is more rewarding.

If one has a gilded soul, one should strive to improve mankind and lift up those who need to change.

If one has a tainted soul, one can only remedy it by sheer determination and effort.

The result will be astounding as you find your "soul" entering a new realm.

A Gun

A gun is a device that fires a projectile and is used as a weapon.

I get so mad; anyone with a gun can do or take anything he wants. Isn't it nice? All you have to do is use it and you do not have to work. You just "take" what you want and from whom you want. Then you can enjoy the spoils.

The "gun" gives people permission to destroy or retrieve anything from anyone they want.

Usually the victims are old and often feeble, which makes the offender feel bigger and stronger with the gun.

I would like to see some of these huge guys with the gun in an arena without the gun facing another culprit with a fight to the finish and see just how brave they are.

Guns should be outlawed and removed from the constitutional right of man. The idea of protection doesn't work. It is used as an offensive, not protective weapon.

It is high time our leaders realized this and did something about it. Presidents have been assassinated and guns still prevail for anyone to have and use.

Anyone can get a gun, legally or illegally, and use it. How lovely? If you have been a victim, as we have, you would feel the way we do. We now have fears.

A lifetime of saving is gone in a ""blink of an eye" and people still say we have rights. Yes, rights for the criminal to plunder and destroy.

Emotions and reactions are now changed.

More police will not correct the criminality, which is progressing by leaps and bounds.

Outlawing guns will cause a big financial savings for the government. Taxes may be reduced. Lives will be saved. It must be fun for a hold-up man to rob and throw an elderly person down. How brave.

War

War can be defined as "battle; a means of settling differences through force."

What a terrible way to end problems, by creating additional problems. The victor gets the spoils; or does he? At what cost? Many people and nations are not satisfied with what they have and are always looking at the other with enmity.

By destruction one does not create. Our Lord created the world for mankind to live together in harmony. There was supposed to be enough for all to survive and develop as we mature.

Unfortunately, men are gregarious individuals, like nations, and are never satisfied with their lot. Perhaps this desire was meant to help develop the world as it grows and make life easier for all. To achieve and enjoy, but, unfortunately, the have-nots want what the haves have and are willing to wage war at the expense of others for their own greed. What is enough? When you, or a nation, are in a comfortable position with plenty to eat and enjoy life, why the desire for more? Is this a characteristic of mankind? Is it greed? Is it the desire to excel? Is it an insecure feeling in men? Is it fear of another nation taking over? There are many reasons that are given and not always the truth, or there would be no soldiers to slaughter.

War is a terrible waste of human beings and property. In the end, at the peace table, the spoils are decided and the victors win.

What a terrible price to pay for rights and land. The vanquished are lost and may never regroup for a proper lifestyle.

"God" should never have allowed such behavior in human beings.

God

God: that which many worship, the Creator of the world, a powerful Being that controls our fate.

We start out in life crying to survive.

Without prior knowledge, we have to make decisions. How many times are we wrong when we try to be right? Do we know right from wrong? We should ask for God's help. Only as we grow and develop and with trial and error are we more apt to be right than wrong.

We must grow and go to school to learn the A,B,C's. As we progress, we must look forward to a life's work. We should not overlook the Lord, as He is a great tranquilizer.

How unfair it is to ask a youngster to decide a future course when he or she has no experience in life's chosen field.

This is where an adult, having gone through a period unknown to a youngster, is so valuable in explaining in simple language what the future might be like, with or without schooling.

We strive for success and wish to be admired for our accomplishment. What is our goal? Does anyone really know?

How far can one go? How far should one go to attain a questionable goal? Most become parents and again they start anew, not knowing how to raise their children. Time is now consumed. We are no longer able to do only what we want, having added responsibility.

Again the unknown—how to raise the youngsters. Later in what field should children be encouraged to follow?

The uncertainty starts all over again. We should ask for "God's" help as he is a great tranquilizer and teacher.

Later most become grandparents and again a new position in life is here.

Some may even become great-grandparents with a lot of love to hold on to.

Time runs out just when one is more knowledgeable and able to help others and make life easier for them. They do not want your advice as you are now old-fashioned.

The new generation must now go through all the trials and tribulations you did. "So be it."

Secure

The dictionary says: 1. Free from danger or harm. 2. Free from care or anxiety. 3. Firmly fixed or fastened. 4. Sure or certain. 5. To get hold or possession of.

We all have doubts.

No one is ever completely secure.

Even the greatest actors and actresses have their doubts prior to going on the stage.

Many become nauseous, develop headaches, and tremble. Many feel choked up or tend to develop a dry mouth or throat. These are only some symptoms because of the insecurity of "man." Imagine a professional golfer trying to win the British Open with a putt of only three feet, which you can make with your eyes closed at any other time.

Tension mounts.

I will now give you an example of how we respond to a simple procedure and how we might conquer our fears.

Put a container, like a small barrel, several feet away from you. Now, toss a ball into the barrel a number of times with ease. Keep doing it for another period of time. As the mouth of the barrel is much larger than the ball, you toss it into the barrel every time. Now, to demonstrate my idea, call in a person to watch you toss the ball into the barrel. You now may become self-conscious and not be quite as sure of yourself that you can do it every time.

Now imagine that you are in a large auditorium full of people with a band playing and you are demonstrating your skill.

Now, pressure is rising, and you are not so sure of yourself. Feelings change again.

To further your anxiety, imagine that there are several tables adjacent to the barrel with crystal glasses filled with water and you are still on the stage with the television camera directed upon you and it's being broadcast all over the world.

Feelings of insecurity mount.

Now, knowing that emotions are involved, you can train yourself to accept people's presence and outside influences and relax by thinking of tossing the ball easily into the barrel.

By testing yourself in different situations, you can become more secure and now realize that only your thinking can make the difference.

Problem

A problem is a dilemma, a difficulty that one must attempt to solve or accept.

Life is full of problems and new ones are forever popping up.

It is often very difficult to face the real problem. We tend to divert our attitude and direction by placing the blame elsewhere or on others as we are not strong enough to face the real problem that confronts us.

This we have to conquer in order to do our best. If we refuse to face problems as they occur, it becomes a sore spot and is a deterrent for progress. We tend to make excuses and accept that which we refuse to face.

I suggest that whatever the problem, in order to reach your best result in this life, you must face the problem. You will benefit and be relieved of anxieties that prevent you from achieving your goal.

To do your best in your life, you must sometimes face the "enemy," which could be your father, mother, boss, wife, husband, and yes, your children. Do not be afraid of the truth. It is better to speak up when you think you are right than to keep quiet and have the problem "eat" you up alive.

If you do not speak out when you feel or even know

you are right, you are harboring a perpetual "enemy" for which you will always suffer. This prevents you from doing your best work. Your ability is now thwarted.

Many great minds have so suffered and been lost because of the failure to face the truth. Only you can come out of this "jail" in your journey through life. You can then achieve your potential and success will be more attainable.

A heavy heart reduces the blood supply to your brain as well as your heart. Blood vessels are constricted and the various organs of the body suffer.

Circulation is impaired.

Now it is up to you. Face it.

Wait

To wait means to hold in abeyance, to serve, or a period during which one holds back or remain motion-less.

What does it really mean?

How does it affect you? Does it cause your blood pressure to rise? Do you become angry when waiting?

Did you ever think how long a second really is?

Can you imagine a world's record in a race depending on less than a second? This is hard to believe, but true.

Split-second timing makes one athlete better than another. Now, if you have to wait in traffic, as we all do, the delay may only be seconds. Do you blow the horn for someone to get out of your way? You may only have to wait at the next signal. What is the rush?

Time is something we all spend and cannot replace. No one likes to wait for another and yet the one who is late often makes a habit of it, which is unfair to the others. One must wait for a term of pregnancy for nine months. This we accept, as it is nature.

So, the next time you have to wait, bring your thoughts to an experience you have enjoyed in the past and relish the time as well spent, even if it is only for a few seconds.

The Psychiatrist

Psychiatry refers to the branch of medicine involved with the study and treatment of mental illness. "Illness comes only from emotions," a psychiatrist said. To prove it was a difficult problem but an idea struck him. He would color water at the source in the city with a harmless lasting bright-colored liquid and observe the consequences. It wasn't long before people thought the water had been tampered by some idiot and was now unsafe.

The newspaper picked up the story and many theories were expounded. One said that it could be a way that "God" was punishing humanity for misbehavior and misconduct.

Another theory was that it might have been a material from outer space; perhaps the UFO's actually existed.

Emergency hospitals were overloaded with sick people with all kinds of ailments and the physicians were unable to help the "injured" with symptoms. Fears made people more docile and friendly as they thought the "end" might be near.

The psychiatrist had triumphed. He called the newspapers to reveal his experiment. But, they would not believe his story. The color gradually disappeared in the water supply and psychological symptoms slowly vanished.

The psychiatrist had proven his point, but no one listened. He became distressed over his failure to convince society that emotions actually can cause illness, so he just withered away.

Effort

Effort refers to trying to achieve something by means of physical or spiritual force.

To progress one must put out the effort.

It is necessary to get a good start.

This means that you must learn as much as you can about the subject or product you are going to work on.

Get all current information available so that you will be apprised of what the result or results may mean or lead to.

You must study hard and apply yourself to the best of your ability. The winner is one whose effort gained new knowledge, not necessarily the one in first place.

Records are broken all the time, and new ideas crop up as you learn, so you should proceed with a will, develop your mind, and be vigorous in your effort for success.

Hate

Hate can be the act, subject, or emotion of intense disliking.

It is only a four-letter word with great amplification. One can say "I hate to get up in the morning," not realizing that they really meant was that they were too lazy or not ready to accept their daily chores. To hate a chore is not the same as to hate someone with enough feeling to inflict great bodily harm.

You may hate your job because you are lazy. Maybe a tough boss is on your tail for one reason or another. On the other hand, you might wake up and say "I am lucky to have a job."

A child might say to a mother or father "I hate you" when asked to pick up his or her clothes or dry the dishes. He/she really means, "I love my parents but hate to do the chores necessary to maintain a lifestyle."

A child may hate his/her teacher or homework but really want to progress without effort. This is not possible. To achieve takes exertion and often a great deal of time, perhaps many years or even an entire lifetime. Any goal worth achieving takes much labor, and the more effort one applies, the easier it becomes, and further progress will be noted. Hate is a protective measure given to mankind for security reasons. You may hate to go out in the dark as you cannot see as well, which would cause you to feel insecure, or fear for your life.

Everyone wants to win in any game. One hates to lose, which is a "normal" feeling.

Certain forms of hate are experienced by all or most people, like loud noises, traffic congestion, filth, poverty with an empty stomach, or an inadequate lifestyle.

One may abhor another just because the other is of a different race, color, or religion. This is wrong, as everyone should be accepted who has good intentions. Man can choose and, as such, should be accepted.

Some of these things that we hate may be improved with effort, thought, and action, and turn into objects of love.

Morose

Synonyms for *morose* include *sullen, sad, gloomy,* and *unhappy.*

Many people get into this feeling and find it difficult to change. It becomes a bad behavioral habit.

What an awful way to start your day.

Pick yourself up and change your attitude.

You are certainly not having fun. If you need emotional security, this is not the way to go. People may feel sorry for you for a certain period of time but will soon leave you.

The idea of a glass half empty or half full certainly applies here. You should try to think of the good qualities that you have and not dwell on the bad.

If you are at school and not doing well, get in there and study. Do your best and do not look at your bad qualities as you tend to exaggerate your faults in your own mind.

Try to curl your lips up into a smile and you will benefit. Look at the sunshine, the flowers, and yes, the sky. Find the blue color and do not look at the dark area.

Life is not always fun, but to be realistic, with effort, you can achieve a better goal and blow the dark clouds away.

Alone

To be alone is to be "by oneself," in isolation, separate from one's fellows.

How horrible to be alone. No one to talk to or confide in. Everyone has some feelings. Some are more sensitive than others. There are times when it is refreshing to be alone, away from outside reality, which gives one a time to think of one's dreams and perhaps plan for the future.

The telephone is one way to contact others, which allows one to verbally get out of one's quarters. This helps while you are conversing, but after the call, you are again alone.

Life is so difficult. You can think of your life as a big business set-up. You certainly need a good staff to have your business run properly. The smart businessman or woman needs assistants and consultants to succeed. You also need consultation with friends and family to enjoy your life to the fullest.

Being detached allows you to think and do as you please, but many problems arise. It is nice to have someone to comfort you and discuss present as well as future problems and events.

If you have been widowed after a lengthy happy

marriage and your partner is no longer available, every decision is now only yours. Every task is multiplied with only you to come to a conclusion. The great loss of a mate affects your thinking and decisions are difficult to make. How terrible to have to make all resolutions. Not only are you brooding, but every task and challenge is now multiplied. You cannot reason very well with a lump in your throat after an exhausting night with little or no sleep to repair your body.

When you are at home, you have "four walls" to view. It's terrible. They don't talk to you. You are now alone. Be good to your mate as they are very valuable and are sorely missed when gone.

Anguish

Anguish means both a terrible pain and to cause terrible anguish.

Note how the word *anguish* itself appears in the second definition.

Could it be that feelings are expressed and cannot be set into words?

It must be so.

The loss of a great mate of sixty-plus years with little time left for the remaining spouse now puts him or her under such strain and stress with tears in abundance.

It becomes hard to swallow.

"The maker" decides who and when to leave this earth. How can the "Almighty" figure that this is an ideal way for couples to end their time on earth?

Aren't we entitled to a better ending than this?

The turnabout lifestyle of the remaining spouse presents a tremendous chore added to the grief and loss of a loving mate.

One's body twists and turns as the sobs return in the day or night and you feel that you cannot breathe. It is difficult to speak as the tears roll down your cheeks. Your body wrenches and twists and turns in an effort to curb them as they tend to destroy your entire being. You can barely speak.

You are told you are lucky to have had such a great spouse for such a length of time and should be satisfied.

Could you be satisfied if you are now alone with four walls to talk to and you realize your mate is not coming to you from the other room? Anguish is the terrible feeling one now feels.

Behavior

We can define behavior as "outward acts."

Our early forms of behavior start out as an infant, never being satisfied, always wanting the mother's breast and even crying for more with adequate milk supply, and proper function on the baby's part.

Obviously if the milk supply is inadequate, this does not apply. The child could be undernourished.

An insecure student may intentionally drop things, forget the homework, or make unusual sounds for attention or employ other methods of attracting attention.

Squeezing a pimple repeatedly is a form of self-destructiveness, which no one will believe. When it eventually heals with a scar, the person often looks for another as there is now a loss of something to do with their hands.

Sulking or crying for attention are usually the acts of an individual who is insecure and needs to be the primary subject.

Wearing tight or outlandish clothes or flaunting nudity is another means of attracting attention. That person wants to be the only subject of conversation.

It is better to get on with one's life: formulate a realistic plan, and go after it. The results will be more lasting and enjoyable. Notice the sky, the trees, the flowers, a small child, and you will be better rewarded than by trying to be the main subject at all times.

Get a new hobby.

Learn to play an instrument. Develop your skills. Meet new people and you will be rewarded with an attractive personality, and you will attract others without even trying. You will have more attention than you could have by being a nuisance.

Cry

Cry means to sob; to yell out; to proclaim; an emotional outburst.

Did you ever cry? Were you ashamed to cry?

By crying there is a release of tension.

Do you feel sorry for yourself?

You cannot change what has already occurred, like spilled milk. A cry-baby wants attention. But do not overlook a person in need. An emotional pain may be greater than any physical pain and last longer, as with the loss of a loved one.

You cannot undo what has already happened, nor bring back the dead.

I do not want you to have to feel morose, but if that be the situation, you have to go on, pick up the pieces, and start anew.

This is easier said than done, but certainly necessary for continued progress.

Take a deep breath, use good sound judgment, see what the situation demands, and go after the best approach that you can. It takes effort, but you can do it.

Crying does not correct a situation.

Remember, if you can, everyone cried when born.

Doomed

When something is doomed, an unhappy future awaits, possibly one including ultimate destruction.

Some say that the world is doomed. This might be true, if one looks at the galaxies with the destructive processes that are going on observable by our modern methods.

A baby born today is doomed to death at a given period of time.

Should that take away your desire to propagate and excel? Should one take for granted that death is inevitable and make that an excuse for not doing our best in our allotted time? We may have many skills to help and enhance mankind and thus feel a purpose for our existence. This could be rewarded by giving us self-satisfaction.

We are often told to be optimistic and do our best at all times. Sounds good. People should feel that they are going to live forever and thus rewards for effort will be forthcoming.

But, when you are the survivor of an excellent marriage and come home alone to four walls, the loss and now being alone cause a depth of feelings that are almost insurmountable as your throat congests and you cannot speak, trying to hold back the tears that flow down your cheeks. You want and often do scream, even at "God." You ask, "Why are we doomed to die?" We have worked hard all our lives to achieve a goal and raise a marvelous family. Why must one leave?

"Is it all worth the effort? For we too will soon be doomed." How tragic.

Different arrangements for life should have been made by our Maker; maybe they are.

Emotions

Emotion encompasses many feelings and states of being possessed by such feelings.

Excitement is one form of emotion in which one can be elated, disturbed, or angered depending on the situation.

Some individuals become excited easily and often to a degree of anger and excess while others are slow to become excited and are more tolerant of situations.

An example: the passing of a flag in a parade brings forward a feeling of belonging to a great country with pride. Unfortunately some adverse groups with antagonistic attitudes may "burn the flag" in an entirely opposite emotion of hate.

Looking forward to a party for a graduate with pride is another type of emotion, one inspired by a job well done.

An honest day's work with sweat and toil may give one a sense of accomplishment, another emotion.

The destitute ones and the failures in this world of plenty arouse a sensation that one cannot justify.

Accomplishment of a goal leads to another goal, etc., which is always a challenge, which many enjoy.

Remember: if you don't try, you cannot succeed. Trying in itself evokes a strong feeling.

Seeing a baby born and taking its first breath brings out untold feelings of disbelief and wonder.

Seeing someone suffer, either from poverty, ill health, or loss of a loved one brings out another feeling, of sadness.

I am getting tired and sleepy, so "good night." Another emotion set down by our "Maker."

Progress, Hope

Progress involves stepping forward, bettering, proceeding toward a desired object, tangible or intangible.

Hope means setting one's mind toward something, no matter what the chances of attaining it are.

After a severe illness or surgery such as by-pass open heart, the victim feels that it is an endless road to recovery. It will never come to pass. The patient is so overwhelmed with all the follow-up examinations and procedures that any progress, if noted, seems so minimal. To await results of tests really tests your emotions.

One suddenly has become a victim and must follow the doctor's orders. Every turn and movement requires a nurse to assist. Calling a nurse tests your waiting ability as every moment seems to take forever. As your body shrinks away and you look in the mirror, it is with disbelief that you realize you are that individual.

You are told you are doing well. You wonder who they are seeing. Encouragement is part of their repertoire.

Nevertheless some improvement begins to occur.

To look to the future and wonder how you will eventually be is paramount in your mind.

The future may not have been unfolded as yet. Ultimately hope is your only weapon. You must give it your all.

Knowledge

Knowledge is the acquaintance with and/or understanding of certain information. Erudition is knowledge gained from reading. Every day of our lives, we are exposed to new things and opportunities. From this we should learn. New vistas are opened. What we do with our learning gives us an opportunity to improve and excel. The brain is nourished, which can lead to further development.

If all one does with the knowledge that is stored in one's brain is to keep it there as in a bank and not put it to good use, it tends to be a loss. Others would benefit, which is a shame. Exchange of ideas can whet the appetite for additional learning.

By contributing facts to the layman as well as the professional, mankind can be benefitted and lead to further development. Certainly we can all stand improvement.

Have a dream and follow that dream.

Remorse

Remorse is regret for past deeds and/or thoughts, often to the point of bitterness.

The way to avoid this is to think good thoughts before you speak. Put yourself in the other person's feelings. This is of course impossible.

Don't downgrade someone to make them feel inferior when in reality you are only trying to build your own ego.

Do unto others as you want done to you is an excellent example of how to avoid these feelings of regret.

Words said in haste and without thought can never be erased and may not even be diminished with time.

Again, to have a good friend is to be a good friend.

The world is full of chaos and nations versus nations have created great trauma. Hopefully, leaders will come along who have a conscience and avoid harm to another. This will have a good effect on people so that they can live together. Remorse will prevail but hopefully be diminished with time.

We can all hope for utopia, but it is my simple belief this will never occur as sisters are often jealous of sisters and brothers of brothers. Since kin cannot avoid problems, causing remorse for misdeeds, jealousies and irritations, so we cannot expect the various countries of different backgrounds and lifestyles to avoid them.

Some of the "great" leaders of the world, past and present, have no compassion, are paranoid, without feelings of remorse. Such are a great menace to mankind. Thus, "remorse" is a great sensation and control that we are endowed with; a deterrent against wrongdoing.

Dreams

Dreams are creations of the imagination, whether created in night or day, often involving extremely vivid imagery.

Dreams are there for everyone.

You can go to the moon. You can go to the sea, to the sky, the mountains—you name it.

From dreams comes progress.

You can climb the highest mountain or swim the deepest river and never leave your abode.

Dreams are for reminiscing, for growth, for development, for invention, and for pleasure. How nice.

You can pretend that you are something or someone—a bird, an airplane—and see how much fun it is to fly or be a fish or a boat and swim or float on the water around the world. Such fantasies are there just for the asking. Pretty nice, I would say.

This is a "God"-given prize. Everyone can have as many as they like without permission from anyone and make their own choices. How nice that we can all have that same privilege, young and old and rich and poor alike.

You can be the greatest comedian or star in your own film, be a king or queen, and even be a rabbit with long ears and jump up and down for fun or be a dog or cat and be petted or bark just for merriment.

I like to dream. I hope you do. It seems like amusement with an escape clause that everyone can enjoy.

Purpose

Purpose is a goal, an expressed desire to meet such a goal, or a reason for something.

We are put on this planet for a purpose.

Each of us has a reason why we were born on this earth. We are not told why, as perhaps in our own individual way we are helping "God" to create a better other world we will eventually enter. He must need our input.

It does not seem right that we are just put on Earth for no good reason. Each is part of a scheme and not told what it is.

We must each have to share the responsibility to develop another better world.

We are now in the school of life and fend for ourselves—groping, struggling often with immense effort to no avail, which is a form of education to bring out the best in us. It is a trial period.

Just as the athlete striving with enormous amounts of exercise and training with self-discipline to be number one in the Olympics, so others do the same in a chosen profession, for good or evil.

There has to be a better world than ours, where we can "all" grow, enjoy, and be in harmony without the evils of mankind on Earth. We are all a part of the next better world we are all striving for, and the effort we put in will reward us in the end and "God" will benefit and accept us with our knowledge gained on this Earth.

According to our behavior here we will be judged in the hereafter, and this should make us realize that the good will prevail and benefit while the tagalongs and evil characters will not be tolerated. They will lose many of the benefits to which the better individuals will be entitled.

What each one contributes, by such will they be judged and be rewarded accordingly.

S-s-s-s-o if in the next world you go to and want the better treatment, you have to earn it in this school on Earth.

There are no freebees there or evils tolerated—it is up to you here and now. "Good luck."

They say, "You can't take it with you"—you certainly do. Your record of deeds on this Earth is yours and only yours.